AF373414

AFTER PAUL CELAN: JOURNEY TO THE TURNING WORD

POETRY AND RELATED PROSE

ALSO BY SHIRLEY GLUBKA

Reflections Caught Leaping: poetry and related prose (2020)

Burst Thought Shall Show Its Root: erasure poetry (2019)

Through the Fracture in the I: erasure poetry (2018)

The Bright Logic of Wilma Schuh: a novel (2017)

End into Opening: six sestinas and their humble companion poems (2014)

Echoes and Links: poems (2013)

Return to a Meadow: a novel (2012)

All the Difference: poems of unconventional motherhood (2012)

Green Surprise of Passion: Writings of a Trauma Therapist (1998)

AFTER PAUL CELAN: JOURNEY TO THE TURNING WORD

POETRY AND RELATED PROSE

SHIRLEY GLUBKA

BLADE OF GRASS PRESS
PROSPECT, MAINE
2020

After Paul Celan: Journey to the Turning Word
poetry and related prose
by Shirley Glubka

paperback

published by:
Blade of Grass Press
85 Bowden Point Road
Prospect, Maine 04981-3000
bladeofgrasspress@gmail.com

Front cover painting:
Luigi Russolo's *House + Light + Sky Movement* (1913)
courtesy of the Art History Project at
arthistoryproject.com/artists/luigi-russolo/house-light-sky-movement

ISBN: 9798558447620

In memory of
Lee Sharkey (1945-2020)
who inspired me to read the work of Paul Celan

with ongoing gratitude to
my bright and faithful manuscript readers—
Laura Levenson
Pauline Duchesneau
Virginia Holmes

CONTENTS

a word with all its green
enters itself, transplants itself

follow it

—Paul Celan

INTRODUCTION

this is about reading—
it is an encounter—
it is inside me in a sort of wildness that finds form—
(from my notes)

It is the middle of the night and I am unable to sleep. I am reading, not for the first time, *The Meridian*, the speech Paul Celan gave to the German Academy for Language and Poetry in 1960 when he accepted the prestigious Georg Büchner Prize. What strikes me as never before is how halting Celan's words are, and how naked—as if this Jewish poet, in a surreal post-Holocaust scene, clutched a small bundle of clothing to his naked body and cautiously picked his way through a nighttime alleyway strewn with broken glass, his feet bare, moonlight exposing his vulnerability; as if he, with great effort, tried simultaneously to make his way toward and escape from an invisible someone or something, saying, "…the poem holds onto the edge of itself…is lonely…wants to reach an Other, it needs this Other…seeks it out, speaks toward it…"

As I sit in my solitude, reading, the moon shining through the skylight, the surrounding sky pure black, I am gripped by an intensity. I might be in Celan's audience, fifteen years after the end of World War II, listening to the words of this man, this poet who will, in less than ten years, leap into the Seine and drown himself. He will be approaching his fiftieth birthday when he dies, just a little younger than my son is now. My heart—naked, exposed—simultaneously clutches itself and reaches out.

Celan continues. "Each human being is a form of this Other." I believe him. I am a form of this Other, an Other he referred to earlier (cautiously, hesitatingly) as "…perhaps…a *wholly Other*."

I close my eyes and breathe into the chilly night air of Ginny's and my much-loved old Maine farmhouse. My heart clutches, reaches—

~~~~~~~~~~

Paul Celan's poems are difficult. They exercise the mind, dig deep into the heart, root around, then turn and escape.

Gone.

Later, on another reading, they might or might not agree to speak.

I had been reading Celan's poems for several years—in translation, I do not read German—when I decided to approach them in a new way. I decided to put what I discovered in his images and thought into lines of my own, "translating" a few of his poems—from English to English. This would be a private exercise, reading through writing.

I only meant to deepen my experience of Celan's poetry but the exercise quickly resulted in something I called "untethered translations" as my writing mind decided to go its own way. I seemed almost to be writing my own poems.

Further along this road I began to think in terms of ekphrasis: as if I stood before a challenging, compelling (often quite abstract) painting and found lines of a poem forming. These lines might begin a poem that became description, interpretation, meditation, or something that flew off quite
~~~~~~~~~~

into its own sky, but always "inspired by," always "after." Always, in other words, rooted in and indebted to a particular poem by Paul Celan.

I wrote twelve poems. I had the bones of a chapbook, but something more was needed. What came was a series of prose responses, one for each of the poems, short companion pieces focused on my way of reading or my way of writing, or on aspects of Celan's biography, or on elements of my own life story.

The project had found its form: twelve poem/prose pairs. I offer them here, deeply conscious of my debt to Paul Celan.

Shirley Glubka
November 2020

EYES, AND THE STANDING HUMAN

—after Paul Celan's "Stehen, im schatten" ("To stand, in the shadow")

There is a sky above
extends to infinity.
It is wounded and healed.

There is a shadow
slashed across earth.
It is the mark of the scar in the sky.

There is a way of standing, alone,
earth-rooted, under the sky,
a way of standing

without words
under the long scar
that shines in the infinite air,

standing in the shadow,
waiting for no one,
enduring the silence,

enduring the shine of the scar,
the immensity,
the eye of the absent god.

On "Eyes, and the Standing Human"—

Celan:

> *To stand, in the shadow*
> *of a scar in the air.*
> —from "To stand, in the shadow"

I turn Celan's image around and around, trying to see it, to know it. I pull at it like taffy, lengthening, softening. Celan uses 31 words for his poem, I use 83.

There are spaces within his poem I cannot find my way to.

We both stand alone. We both, though we are writing, are without words.

His tiny poem enlarges itself until it reaches, "even without / language" to "all that has room in it." This is beyond me.

I stand earth-rooted. Where does he stand? We are not told.

My poem has a god, absent but explicit. There is no god in his poem.

My scar, which appears several times, shines in infinite air. Celan's scar, appearing once, casts a shadow from its place the air. That is all we know.

FOLLOW THE TRACES

—after Paul Celan's "Engfürung" ("Stretto")

Grass-blades, trampled by the long forced walk,
slowly pull themselves upright,
bright green against white stones—

silent determined beautiful white stones,
sunlight stunning them,
the strict field calling, displaying its realities.

Crushed green words warily right themselves—
cautious difficult labor,
necessary repetition, remembrance.

Sunlight draws particles of time toward evening,
toward night: gathered armloads,
the real, the unreal, disentangling, transfiguring—

clear-cut forms, luminous hues, geometry of visions,
sky-held, visible only when grass-blades,
almost upright—when striving word-blades—disappear.

On "Follow the Traces"—

Celan:

Taken off into
the terrain
with the unmistakable trace:

Grass, written asunder. The stones, white
with the grassblades' shadows...
. . .

Circles,
red or black, bright
squares, no
flight shadow...
—from "Stretto"

I can only work with the tiniest parts of Celan's 514-word "Stretto," a major poem. It is as if I focus on the detail of a large painting and write an ekphrasis.

Ghosts of the Holocaust hover over Celan's poem, his mother shot by Nazis, his father dying of illness in the death camp. There is nothing like this in my own history. Nothing.

My grass-blades are green, bright. My strong stones are beautiful in sunlight, determined.

We both work for our words. We both come through to visions. I echo, conscious of my limited capacity.

APOLOGIA FOR THE EYE OF JOY

—after Paul Celan's "Ein Auge, Offen" ("An Eye, Open")

> *"Do not look away," pleaded the victims.*
> *—Edmond Jabès, The Book of Questions*

Where, for the inexplicably blessed, is the salt tear,
sliced by reality, through which clear sight comes?

Inside the wound of another,
depths of mystery, darkness revered.

We for whom light is a familiar, who can only offer
attention, which is a form of prayer, almost see.

Then comes joy, stumbling behind,
wishing to keep up, not meaning to interfere—

solemn earnest awkward joy—
joy with its eye, holding itself open,

yearning for unearned acuity,
for the second half of the split tear.

On "Apologia for the Eye of Joy"—

Celan:

> *The tear, half of it,*
> *a sharper lens, nimble,*
> *brings you images.*
> —from "An Eye, Open"

It is Juneteenth, 2020. George Floyd's death at the end of May is much on our minds: death of a Black man—a knee on his neck, a sort of lynching by the police—filmed by helpless bystanders.

Around the world: gatherings, protests. At the same time, the pandemic.

Death and death.

I sit and write my poem.

Celan's tear, but only half of it, becomes a sharper lens. I make of this what I can from my inexplicably blessed perspective. The joy of shaping language, the joy of seeing light, in the midst.

Apologia: the word is not meant to indicate a well of shame in the psyche of the fortunate. It is meant as a defense of, a speaking on behalf of. For I appreciate the eye of joy.

VOICE OF THE MOTHER WHO SUFFERED,
                    AND PASSED INTO DEATH

—after Paul Celan's "Nähe der Gräber" ("Nearness of Graves")

When large crimson waters moved through me,
roiling as if wounded,

the banks and fields of my soul gave way
in silent surrender to solace.

Speak you therefore, child,
your own living word.

On "Voice of the Mother Who Suffered, and Passed into Death"—

Celan:

> *And can you bear, Mother, as once on a time,*
> *the gentle, the German, the pain-laden rhyme?*
> *—from "Nearness of Graves"*

Celan's early poem—so unlike those he was to write later: this one explicit, even rhymed—addresses his mother. As always, he writes in German. Can she bear it? Can he? German is the language his mother loved but it is a ruined language, tool of the Nazis, who killed her.

Beyond death, Celan's mother gives full permission. Yes, my poem insists, she can bear it. And he must.

Celan ends another poem—his "*Kleide die Worthöhlen aus*" ("Line the wordcaves")—with this admonition:

> *listen for their second*
> *and each time second and second*
> *tone.*

He is writing a brief *ars poetica*, most likely reminding himself to listen to his own words in this attentive way. I am a mother and a daughter. I find myself listening to the poem I have written in the voice of a mother, a mother very different from my own mother and from me. I think of our safe American lives, our Catholic roots, but still—

Second tones—

My mother, unlike Celan's, died in very old age. She suffered, as ordinary humans do, but that is ended. She consistently applauded my written words, no matter where they went. I think of her now, tell her I have a new poem. Her eyes light up.

I am the mother of a grown child who, from the age of three, was raised by another mother. This was my choice, I was not made for the work of ongoing daily parenting. My son, good man, accepts—accepts his reality, accepts my reality, accepts and even sometimes reads what I've written about my experience as an "unconventional mother," the fiction, poetry, essays. Someday he might have words of his own, beyond acceptance, to say, or to write—

Speak you, therefore, child…

SNOW, BLOOD, KEY

—after Paul Celan's "Mit Wechselndem Schlüssel"
                                    ("With a Changing Key")

If each time you unlock the house
where indoor snow floats and falls

(you: seeking the silenced,
the shape-shifting word;

word drifting hidden
in unsteady eye-testing snow)

blood gathers and spurts in its need
to be seen, to be heard, to be said,

but you are unable or only partially able
to see or hear or say—

if the word itself must be born
again and again—

it is fortunate that the key
which unlocks the house where the word is

also changes repeatedly, now worn thin,
now nearly fresh-cut. On this day,

when the wind of your world lacks mercy,
the changed key is still rough, not yet

smoothed to the lock. You will have time
to toughen your mind while you work the

recalcitrant lock before blood gathers
and bursts and flows around the melting,

radiant ice of the newborn word which you
glimpse but cannot touch, cannot hold.

On "Snow, Blood, Key"—

Celan:

> *With a changing key*
> *you unlock the house where*
> *the snow of what's silenced drifts.*
> *Just like the blood that bursts from*
> *your eye or mouth or ear,*
> *so your key changes.*
> —from "With a Changing Key"

Celan's poem: 58 words. My poem: 157 words.

My words wind around and around Celan's surreal yet elemental images until shape comes for me, and sense, and I find I have a poem.

Shape and sense: which now, as reader of my own words, and of Celan's, I grasp and lose repeatedly.

The strangeness strikes me: reader and writer in separate private moments watch the birth of a poem. Later, in other moments, the same poem is born again, from the work of both reader and writer. Born differently.

Human making seems a living tapestry, bright red threads of human suffering strung swiftly through some vast icy universal radiance emerging from the dark.

AFTER STRIVING

i.

When you awake, the stone is only a stone,
itself, separate, though wavering under the water.

The circle the word made over the stone
has left a faint shadow. This is a courtesy.

The tree has righted itself, roots in dry soil,
limbs flinging worship.

The enigmatic beads are rolling,
the string of the necklace is broken.

The crumb at the center remains,
shaped like the eye of a witnessing god.

ii.

Alone, each piece refuses to fit.
Each single outline insists. Each
unique shape stubbornly settles
into itself. Look then to the spaces,
allow them their moveable un-shapes.
Listen to them vibrate in silence
or whisper as they disappear into
spinning pools under moonlight,.
You will feel the long urge of time

stretching, and dream-breathe your own
merciful momentary far-reaching whole.

On "After Striving"—

Celan:

> *...a stone in the water and a circle*
> *and over the water a word...*
> —from "I Heard It Said"

My title expresses my bewilderment. Why did Celan put these particular images together in his succinct but apparently disjunct 13-line poem? There is a stone in the water, an upside down tree, a chain of judgments, a crumb shaped like someone's eye.

I find myself reading and rereading, striving toward some sort of unity. This might be a matter of rowing against Celan's tide. I write my own determined, perhaps stubborn, solution. "Look…. Listen…. You will feel…" This will become my second stanza.

Next I write what will be my first stanza, doing what I apparently must do, image by image, a matter of reading-through-writing; or writing-through-reading. This. And this. And this. Celan's stone, water, circle, word; his tree; his chain; his crumb in the shape of an eye. I make each one mine. I insist on couplets, which is not the form Celan used. I arrive at a witnessing god.

Celan, the exile, arrives at a tree he can no longer see. The final line of his poem is: "And saw my poplar no more." Commentators tell me the poplar stands for the Jewish people. Earlier in the poem he did see: "I saw its roots pray heavenward for night."

We are such different writers, Celan and I. Or is there something…? Whose eye is that, in Celan's poem? Who gives shape to his crumb?

NAKED AND ANCIENT

—after Paul Celan's "Welchen Der Steine Du Hebst" ("Whichever Stone You Lift")

Reach for the word floating on flames,
hermetic word, long imprisoned
within the burning, fragile structure.

Remember the bed, carved from cut trees,
where you lay on assumed solidity,
the bed which was and was not.

Here is the stone you must lift.
Unburned, warmed by flame,
it has lain in its place all your life.

Innocent forms caught embracing
slither forth, naked and ancient,
over the elemental earth.

On "Naked and Ancient"—

Celan:

> *Whichever stone you lift—*
> *you lay bare*
> *those who need the protection of stones:*
> *naked,*
> *now they renew their entwinement…*
>
> *Whichever word you speak—*
> *you owe to*
> *destruction.*
> —from "Whichever Stone You Lift"

Celan's poem starts with his stone. There are no flames in his poem, no burning structures, unless hidden in the crevices, or in the history.

We both place a bed in the middle. His is (mysteriously, to me) one "where / souls are stayed once again." The existential status of these beds—these structures one might lie down on, rest on—is uncertain.

I work my way to the stone, and to the naked ones exposed when the stone is lifted, to their embracing forms.

"Whichever stone you lift" is the only poem, I learn, in which Celan uses the word "Destruction." It is a word for the Holocaust. Elsewhere, Celan speaks and writes of the Holocaust only as "that which happened."

"Destruction" is the final word of his poem, the reality to which he owes his words, his life work. I end with my innocent forms, with my elemental earth. Little earthworms are what I see. Living, wriggling beings.

Are Celan's entwined forms alive? I cannot escape the piles of bodies thrown together in the camps, have to remind myself again and again of their *renewed* entwinement in Celan's poem.

Suddenly, having read his poem many times, having written my own poem in response, I see not only the starved dead human bodies but also the mangled words of the German language. Celan's work is the work of resurrection: "Naked / now they renew their entwinement."

JOURNEY TO THE TURNING WORD

—after Paul Celan's "Sprich Auch Du" ("Speak You Too")

When the light is high and the shadow
contracts, do not stand waiting.

Stretch upward with ardor into the limitless,
a long journey. Night will arrive.

A star will appear which you will touch.
Carefully carry the desiring star,

carry it downward along the slender thread
you have become,

carry it to open water where for the first time
it saw itself. The yearning star

wants to leap and dive
with splashing young syllables,

offspring of the turning word,
the kaleidoscopic word

forever forming, moving
into and out of,

now near and
now far,

dark unto death

and erupting to glory—

Word
which is—

is the you—
is the I—
is the Other.

On "Journey to the Turning Word"—

Celan:

> *But now the place shrinks, where you stand.*
> *Where now, shadow-stripped, where?*
> *Climb. Grope upwards.*
> *Thinner you grow, less knowable, finer!*
> *Finer: a thread*
> *the star wants to descend on:*
> *so as to swim down below, down here*
> *where it sees itself shimmer: in the swell*
> *of wandering words.*
> —from "Speak You Too"

It is the thread that catches me first, then this entire final stanza of Celan's "Speak You Too." My poem materializes, but without working the center of Celan's poem, which is: "Speak— / But don't split off No from Yes."

I want to work with that center. I try again and again, but I am unable. Celan said it. I can't take it apart, I can't add. This is a pattern: I can never quite "translate" Celan. There is so much white space—the absence that hovers. There is always more.

Celan ends with wandering words. I find myself with a turning word. My turning word is Celan's, though: his you, his thou, which turns and turns.

Except that I am explicit—there is a questionable tightness to the final stanza of my poem, a lack of white space. I see this, but find I need to leave the lines as they are. Sometimes this happens.

ALWAYS TAKING PLACE

—after Paul Celan's "Wirk nicht voraus" ("Do not work ahead")

> *"With the shift from essence to existence as the first principle of*
> *metaphysics,*
> *we can say that there is always more."*
> —David Mutschlecner, *Poetic Faith*

> *"...the newness is always in poetry exploring the ways*
> *to sing the more in reality that has always taken place."*
> —Robert Kaufman, Introduction to *Under the Dome:*
> *Walks with Paul Celan*, by Jean Daive

The newness—
the more—

but we must never yearn
beyond the moment
of our own footprint,

nor may we covet
the made word
given from deeper in time,

but must stand alone
in this unmarked place

and wait for
our own pinprick
through which
the needle of light,

stitching the rip,

(the needle moving,
pinprick by pinprick,
revealing, concealing,
as we stand unmoving,
in this place,
pierced by the needle
which knows
and says
without saying,
but knowing)

once again offers,
unresting, insisting, desiring,
the word become thou.

On "Always Taking Place"—

Celan:

> *Do not work ahead,*
> *do not send abroad,*
> *stand*
> *in here:*
>
> *deep-grounded by Nothingness,*
> *free of all*
> *prayer…*
> —from "Do not work ahead"

I am reading Gershom Scholem's *Major Trends in Jewish Mysticism* and come to the Kabbalist idea of En-Sof, the hidden god, the god-before-God. No trace of anthropomorphism. Good. I read on. Scholem writes of the transformation of En-Sof, "the inexpressible fullness, into nothingness."

I am also reading John Felstiner's biography of Celan. I learn that Celan, who sometimes called himself an atheist, who was raised in an Orthodox Jewish family, who seems to me to have written himself into his own agonized and somehow deeply joyful spirituality, a spirituality with a very Jewish flavor, read Scholem, and met him.

Celan's Nothingness, where we are "free of all / prayer" suddenly makes sense. This is the place (the non-place) where prayer makes no sense, where we can only stand naked. Petition is pointless. There is no god to pray to. Celan is with the god-before-God.

Still, in their final stanzas, both Celan's poem and mine offer some sort of addressable presence. His: "you I take up / in place of all / rest." Mine: "the word become thou."

I needed a needle to get there, a needle to work me, pinprick by pinprick, in and out, in and out. Celan refrains from describing a process, if there is one. He stands in Nothingness, he takes up his you.

THAT WHICH HAS EVER BEEN

*—after Paul Celan's "Das Wort vom Zur-Tiefe-Gehn" ("The word about
going to the depths")*

It is my place to say the small thing,
but even the small thing holds in its little cup

an infinity of depth which can bubble forth,
gently blown upward by one who swims

through youth and through age, the same god,
now elusive, now evident, known and strange.

On "That Which Has Ever Been"—

Celan:

> *The word about going-to-the-depths*
> *that we once read.*
> *The years, the words since that.*
> *We're still just that.*
> —from "The word about going to the depths"

Theorists have been wrestling with the concept (or metaphor) of depth for quite some time. When I went to graduate school in my fifties and found myself reading literary theory I discovered that not everyone was in love with depth, not everyone longed for that experience. There seemed to be a new devotion to a certain flatness. I never understood this. Decades later, I am unworried about flatness. I smile, resonating with Celan's "We're still just that." I write my small poem.

I see that I am unable to write myself into the largeness Celan creates as his poem continues: "…no end of space … you don't need to fly … what inscribed itself in your eye / deepens our depth." Always Celan seems to say more, open more space around (or into?) his words. Why "your eye," but "our depth"? Who is the you? Who are we?

Celan's "We're still just that" seems to say, "Well, here we are, we haven't really gone anywhere, have we?" A moment of insight, written with wry humility? Maybe. Also, I think, a statement made seriously. Owned.

My poem makes its own discovery. "Here it is, a god in my psyche. Apparently it was there all along." Are we writing the same moment, Celan and I? Well, probably not precisely the same moment. But there is kinship.

THEN WOULD BE

—after Paul Celan's "Entwurf einer Landschaft"
("Sketch of a Landscape")

If we traveled back through mythic seasons
and lowered ourselves to the ridge of the
deep round grave-hole time dug

and waited for the beginning
when light was allowed
and rock-eruption was allowed

(stunned rocks upward-thrust
to air's strange visibility,
to existence)—

if we then breathed
and waited, silent, each from a place,
and saw into the clear burning crater

and humbly spoke, one after another,
our single, given, upthrust crystal-word,
then would be, each; then would be all.

On "Then Would Be"—

Celan:

> *Round graves, below. In*
> *four-beat the year's pacing*
> *on steep steps around them.*
>
> *Lava, basalt, worldheart-*
> *red-heated stone…*
> *where light formed for us before*
> *breath…*
> —from "Sketch of a Landscape"

Celan's "landscape" builds. It is complex, daunting. I let go of trying gather it all up.

I meditate on particular elements. The graves. Time. The volcano. The light. The breath.

I feel silence, an imperative to wait, a sense of my own small place, a sort of necessity—as if appointed, or gently mandated. I am to stay exactly here, among all others.

I find myself in a state of longing.

Then the crystal word, the gratitude.

And again the longing.

EPILOGUE: WITH SECOND SOUL AND ONE OTHER

—after Paul Celan's "Mit Allen Gedanken" ("With all my thoughts")

A task, to lug a lifetime's thought
and nothing else,
to leave the world I know.

But you appear and take us in,
my thoughts and what remains of me,
a bundle of old efforts and uncertainty.

You are the one unpacks my thoughts,
tells me to rest. I close my eyes.
A second soul stands with me now.

We stand like strangers, hand in hand,
strong enough to make a silence
over which the light must come,

a light we two will shape,
mysterious work, but ours,
while you look on.

On "Epilogue: With Second Soul and One Other"—

Celan:

> *With all my thoughts I went*
> *right out of the world: there you were,*
> *you my gentle one, you my open one, and—*
> *you took us in…*
>
> *Huge, a sun came drifting, bright*
> *against it stood soul and soul, clear…*
>
> *Easily, / your womb opened…*
> —from "With all my thoughts"

I am nervous, trying to write my "ekphrastic" response to this poem by Celan. The erotic imagery feels decidedly heterosexual and male. I am neither. But I'm drawn to that little phrase, "soul and soul." I think of Eros, of Plato: the human sex act reaches beyond itself, the erotic is everywhere.

By the time his poem is complete Celan has gone to the far reaches of "making" and to what is "as good as a name." I think of the crucial (creative) act of naming in Kabbalist thought. I think, too (always at the age of 78 I am thinking of these things) of the final stages of life, of death, of some mysterious possible existence after death.

I take what I can from Celan and prepare to write my own poem. Here is my little suitcase, it needs unpacking. Someone appears—"you"—and takes care of that, instructing me to rest. A second soul appears. A stranger, with whom I hold hands.

Writing this poem, reading and rereading it later, I have an ongoing sense of mystery, or perhaps oddity. Who is the "you"? Who (or what) is the "second soul"?

Sometimes it seems the "you" of this poem is you, reader. The same (my latest rereading of my own poem suddenly tells me) might even be true, or truer, of the "second soul." You, reader, might be my second soul.

And—because the words gently and repeatedly turn—something or someone *wholly Other* might also be there, in the "you" or even in the "second soul." Yes, that too.

KEY WORKS RELIED ON

Celan, Paul. *Selected Poems and Prose of Paul Celan*, translated and with an introduction by John Felstiner, W.W. Norton, New York and London. 2001.

Celan, Paul. *Breathturn into Timestead: the Collected Later Poetry*, Bilingual Edition, translated from the German with commentary by Pierre Joris. Farrar, Straus and Giroux, New York. 2014

Felstiner, John. *Paul Celan: Poet, Survivor, Jew*, Yale University Press, New Haven and London. 1995.

Scholem, Gershom, *Major Trends in Jewish Mysticism*, foreword by Robert Alter, Schocken Books, New York. 1946, 1954, 1974. Foreword copyright 1995.

Jabès Edmond, *The Book of Questions, Volume I*, translated by Rosmarie Waldrop, Wesleyan University Press, Middleton, CT. 1972-1991.

Also: There is a cornucopia of material on the life and work of Paul Celan readily available on the internet, including alternative translations of his poems and prose, as well as material on related poets and writers such as Ingeborg Bachmann, Martin Buber, Edmond Jabès, Osip Mandelstam, Nelly Sachs, Gershom Scholem, and Margarete Susman. I dipped into a good deal of this and am indebted to all who thus share their work.

NOTES ON TRANSLATION

Quotations of Celan's poetry and prose are from John Felstiner's translations in *Selected Poems and Prose of Paul Celan.*

Two exceptions: The epigraph to this collection (*"a word with all its green enters itself, / transplants itself // follow it"*) is translated by Pierre Joris, as is *"listen for their second / and each time second and second / tone"* in the prose on "Voice of the Mother Who Suffered, and Passed into Death."

The quote from Edmond Jabès (epigraph to "Apologia for the Eye of Joy") is translated from the French by Rosmarie Waldrop.

ABOUT THE AUTHOR

Shirley Glubka was born in Washington, D.C. in 1942. She is a retired psychotherapist, the author of two novels, a full-length poetry collection, four poetry chapbooks, and three mixed-genre collections. Her prose and poetry have been published in various journals, online and in print, and in a number of anthologies. She lives in Prospect, Maine with her spouse, Virginia Holmes.

For a generous online sampling of Shirley's ekphrases, a favorite form—
The Ekphrastic Review:
http://www.ekphrastic.net/apps/search?q=glubka

For much more—
Website: https://shirleyglubka.weebly.com

To contact Shirley—
bladeofgrasspress@gmail.com